THE
Old Photographs
SERIES

AROUND
SHIREBROOK

The Hollies, 1934. Mr Hardy, gardener to the Thompson family, pictured in the garden of 'The Hollies' in 1934. With him are the black labradors that were the pets of Lucy and Ethel, Mr Thompson's twin daughters.

THE Old Photographs SERIES

AROUND SHIREBROOK

Compiled by
Geoff Sadler

ALAN SUTTON

BATH • AUGUSTA • RENNES

Alan Sutton Limited
12 Riverside Court
Bath BA2 3DZ

ISBN 0 7524 0028 2

Typesetting and origination by
Alan Sutton Limited
Printed in Great Britain by
Redwood Books, Trowbridge

Rifle Drill, Park Road. A group of unknown Shirebrook volunteers muster for rifle drill in the garden of Hope House, home of Dr H.W. Joyce, on Park Road. Dr Joyce, the local physician during the First World War, held a commission in the Territorial Army, which may explain the location. In the background are the embankment and railway bridge crossing Park Road itself, which were built as part of the Leen Valley Extension in the 1900s.

Contents

Acknowledgements

First thanks must go to Stanley Bettison and Malcolm Shaw, for the loan and reproduction of items from their collections, and from that of Malcolm's father, the late Henry Shaw. These gentlemen have rendered a valuable service to Shirebrook historians by depicting the village and its inhabitants during the 1950s, and between them provided almost one quarter of the photographs in this book.

Sincere thanks are also expressed to the following, for kind permission to reproduce their photographs here:

Mr J. Allsop, Mr A. Ashton, Mrs H. Barke, Mr D. Belcher, Mrs K. Bell, Mr G. Bradbury, Mr J. Brett, Mr A. Burden, Mr and Mrs S. Chessel, Mr F.C. Cooke, Mrs D. Cowlishaw, Mr E.H. Gilbert, Mr W. Glover, Mr S. Grainger, Mr E. Hardy, Mr George Harrison, Mr M. Howson, Mrs R. Jarrett, Mrs D. Leadbeater, Mr L. Lee, Mr Barry Lyons, Mrs J.M. Madin, Mr J. McKenzie, Mr R. Mee, Mrs M. Moore, Mr D. Neale, Mr M.J. Newham, Mrs C. Nicholson, Mrs Nuttal, Mr C.J. Oakton, Mrs A.G. Payne, Mrs J. Pegg, Mr Eddie Pitchford, Mrs K. Ragsdale, Mr H. Robinson, Mrs T. Swincoe, Mr H. Theakstone, Mrs B. Thompson, Mr J. Tomlinson, Mr R. Walker, Mr Ken Wagstaff, Mrs N. Watkinson, Mr E. Wheeler, Mr Herbert "Pommer" Wilson, Mr Ray Wilson, Mrs H. Wood, Mr W.W. Young, Mr Jeremy Plews and Mansfield "Chad", Mr K. Beeston and British Coal, Mr J. Wheeton, Miners' Rescue Station, Mansfield Woodhouse, *Sheffield Star*.

For information and advice, thanks to:

Mr R. Brewster, Mr D. Crute (Mansfield Local Studies Library), Mr J.S. Fowler, Mr D. Lee, Mr and Mrs P. Liversidge, Mr E. Lomax, Mr J. McKenzie, Mrs R. Ramsden, Miss J. Reddish, Mrs M. Reddish, Mr Stan Searl, Mansfield Town F.C. historian, Mr Billy Simons, Records Secretary, Sunderland F.C., Mr Ernest Smith, Mr Tony Warrener.

Thanks to the members of the Shirebrook & District Local History Group, many of whom provided photographs from their own collections, and all of whom gave valuable support:

Miss E. Adams, Mrs M. Bramley, Mr H. Chapman, Mrs P. Doan, Mr A. Hallam, Mr C. Hawley, Mr J. Mallett, Mr D. Middleton, Mr G. Naylor, Mr E. Roberts, Mrs J. Sadler, Mr R. Scruby, Mr K. Walker.

Finally, thanks to Dave Robert for the Ezra Read album cover. And if anyone who should appear here has been omitted, I hope they will accept my apologies.

VE Day Parade, 1945. A soldier leads the oddly-assorted procession, appropriately along Victoria Street, as Shirebrook celebrates the end of the war in Europe.

Introduction

This book is not "a history of Shirebrook." Others have taken on that particular task over the past years, and although the full story of the village remains untold, there have already been a number of significant contributions. Trevor Skirrey's pioneering efforts in the late 1960s and 1970s deserve close attention, and the likes of S.O. Kay, K.F. Mills, P.J. Ibbotson and John Steel have provided further insights. More recently, Charles Crapper's extensive and painstaking research into the pre-industrial village and its nature, detailing the settlement and its inhabitants at the time of the 1748 Enclosure Act, has added a new perspective to Shirebrook's past, while Ernest Roberts and myself have made a close study of the early history of the colliery. For the reader in search of dates and events, these are the places to look.

Shirebrook was a farming settlement that grew suddenly and violently to ten times its normal size when the colliery was sunk in the late 1890s. From that time to the present, with that same colliery awaiting its final destruction, the man with a camera has been part of Shirebrook life, rendering the village and its past immortal with images of streets and buildings and people. This book is a celebration of the past hundred years in visual form, and its two hundred photographs range from business publicity shots to the efforts of the wandering amateur, from professional portraits to holiday family snaps. Insofar as "every picture tells a story", it might reasonably be described as a social history in pictures, which hopefully shows the village in its many and varied aspects.

In the course of compiling this work I have been made aware of two important facts, one encouraging, the other less so. This book has taught me what a marvellous treasure-house of photographs has lain out there "undiscovered" for so long, tucked away in the homes of Shirebrook people. To those who regard their old family snapshots, or those of their parents and grandparents, as so much rubbish to be thrown away, I would urge them to do no such thing. Those images are history, and as such they are of value to local historians; they should be valuable to you, too! The exhibitions held locally by the Shirebrook & District Local History Group have demonstrated the significance of photographs of this kind, and the interest they generate in Shirebrook people of all ages. If you have no use for your old pictures, you may be sure that there are others in Shirebrook who do. Please pass them on, or at least allow copies to be taken, before you dispose of them. Who knows, they may be the sole surviving images of a lost street or building, or a long-dead local character, and as such their one hope of immortality.

Altogether more saddening has been the awareness that time and again I have had to write "this building has since been demolished." Shirebrook has already lost far too many of its historic buildings. The old Council Yard Depot came down in 1992, and very soon the Shirebrook Colliery complex and the Town Hall will follow. Perhaps we should be thankful that other uses have been found for the old Congregational Church, and the School House, to say nothing of the "Gate" Inn. All of these three ought to be listed buildings, nor are they alone. At a time when so much of the village's heritage has been destroyed, it is surely even more important for us to preserve what remains.

Much of that past heritage may be glimpsed in the photographs that fill the following pages. I hope that those who read on will recall those times with pleasure and affection, and if you cannot remember them, maybe - like me - you will learn something about Shirebrook as it was.

And for those of you who mutter about books being full of mistakes. Don't mutter, come out of the woodwork and tell me what they are!

Geoff Sadler

12.7.94

One
The Village

Old Vicarage and School House, Main Street. A turn of the century shot which reveals Main Street as an unmade stretch of road separating the two Victorian buildings that were landmarks of the old farming village. The Vicarage, skylined on the far side of the road, was built in 1855 at a cost of £700. The School House, a National School first erected in 1852, appears at the edge of the picture on the right, and is still in use as a restaurant.

Old Vicarage, Main Street. A close-up view of the vicarage, this time from the other side. The building served as a home for several noted Shirebrook clergymen, among them the keen antiquary Rev. John Cargill, the redoubtable Father Braddon whose thirty-eight years in office saw the growth of the modern village, and the Rev. A.H. Hurt, whose famous actor son John Hurt spent his childhood in Shirebrook. None of these associations was enough to save the Victorian structure, which was demolished and replaced by a modern vicarage in the 1960s.

Main Street, 1950s. A view from the western, Warren Terrace side, showing the railway bridge spanning Main Street. Originally constructed as part of the Great Northern Railway's Leen Valley Extension, the bridge was removed during the 1970s.

Main Street, 1950s. The same bridge, this time seen from the eastern side. In the foreground Main Street follows a sharp bend as it continues into the centre of the village, while on the left is the junction with Central Drive, part of the Model Village built by the Shirebrook Colliery Company from the 1890s onwards.

Main Street and Old Council Yard, 1950s. Main Street enters Shirebrook from the west, linking with King Edward Street and Portland Road to form a central route through the village. Here it approaches the junction of Byron Street (left) and Church Drive (right). The converted stone farm buildings on the right, formerly the council depot, were demolished in 1992.

Old stone houses, Main Street. These buildings are relics of the old farming settlement, and may well date back to the eighteenth century. They are currently threatened with demolition.

Strutt's Yard, off Main Street, c. 1923.
A cluster of stone houses built to the
right of Main Street in 1780, Strutt's
Yard later became one of the more run-
down areas of Shirebrook, and was
eventually demolished in 1936. The
house shown is No.7, home of the
Oakton family who came to the village
when the colliery was sunk in 1896. The
child in the pram is the late Ivan
Oakton.

Grainger & Son, Main Street. Charles
Grainger established his house decorating
business at 47 Main Street in the 1920s. It
later became a hardware shop whose
extended premises included the former
bakery of Harry Thompson on Nicholson's
Row. Charles Grainger is in the doorway, his
son Harold by his bicycle outside, while Mrs
Mabel Grainger appears in the window on
the left.

Byron Street, 1950s. Taken at a junction with Main Street. In the foreground to the left is the old Shirebrook Fire Station building, replaced by the present station on Portland Road in 1986, and beyond it the railway bridge. The man crossing the road is Fred Spencer, who worked as a gravedigger at the cemetery.

Back of Byron Street, 1950s. A rear view of the street from the same period, providing a closer sight of the Fire Station building and the row of houses opposite.

Joseph Paget's grave, parish churchyard. Joseph Paget was the village squire and a major landowner, who occupied nearby Stuffynwood Hall from the 1850s onwards. Perhaps the most important figure in the old agricultural village, he died in 1896, the year the colliery was sunk, and is buried to the rear of the parish church.

Sarah Wildgoose's grave, parish churchyard. Sarah Wildgoose was the servant of John and Elizabeth Nicholson, members of an important family of Shirebrook. The inscription describes her as "of the Nicholson family".

Congregational Church altar, Model Village. Erected in 1905, the Congregational Church was the largest religious edifice in the Model Village proper, and in its heyday accommodated 300 worshippers. The impressive stone building still dominates the summit of Church Drive, although nowadays it has a more secular use as a social club. This picture from its days of glory shows the altar, and in the background the imposing pipe organ.

Baptist chapel, Model Village. One of several non-conformist chapels built in the Model Village in the early part of this century. This wooden structure was the second version, replacing an earlier Baptist chapel demolished in 1914, which has itself long disappeared.

Salvation Army chapel, Byron Street. Built in 1899, the Salvation Army hut faced the parish church across the road from the junction of Byron Street and Main Street. It has since been demolished, and replaced by a modern Salvation Army Hall on a fresh site.

Shirebrook Cemetery, Pleasley Road c.1900. Following a typhoid outbreak in the late 1890s, when the churchyard became overcrowded with victims buried close to the surface, Shirebrook Cemetery site was purchased in 1899. This view from an old postcard shows the cemetery in its early days.

Seen from above: Holy Trinity church. A stunning aerial view of the parish church, taken in 1954 or 1955. The outline of the Victorian church, first opened for worship in 1844 and now a listed building, is superbly caught, together with the churchyard and its scattered headstones. In front of the church are the cenotaph and the Church Hall, while the old Council Yard

buildings (now demolished) may be seen across the road. Between the buildings and the church itself, Church Drive curves down to join Main Street on its eastward journey through the village.

Hollycroft Farm, off Main Street. Built in the 1680s, this building has at various times been the "Blue Bell" Inn, serving the coach traffic from Pleasley during the 18th century, and a farmhouse for the Stockdale family. It has now been converted for residential use by Mr Brian Mitchell.

Hollins' mill, Pleasley Vale. William Hollins founded his textile mill in Pleasley Vale, a short distance from Shirebrook, in the 1780s. The first industrial employer of Shirebrook labour, he gave work to large numbers of men and women before the arrival of the colliery, and thereafter remained the chief employer of local female labour. This 1980s picture shows the mill shortly before it was abandoned and allowed to fall derelict.

Derbyshire's outfitters, 55 Main Street. Andrew Derbyshire was in business as a draper at 55 Main Street in 1908, and his claim to be the oldest outfitter in Shirebrook may well be correct. Sadly, he did not remain in operation for long, and had disappeared from local directories by 1916.

Ernest J. Latham, Main Street. One of the oldest Shirebrook businesses, the chemist's shop established by Ernest J. Latham at 71 Main Street in 1899 continued to prosper until comparatively recent times, but has now been demolished. The reference to photographic goods is of some interest, as Ernest Latham took several photographs of the village.

E.T. Bright, painter & decorator, Station Road. Operating in 1908 under the management of Miss Louie Bright, the painting and decorating business at 113 Station Road was later inherited by Edwin Thomas Bright who is shown behind his counter backed by rolls of wallpaper. From the mid-1920s onwards the address became 225 Market Place, and new premises were later found at 5 King Edward Street.

G.R. Jones, King Edward Street. Framed in the shop doorway, George Robert Jones poses beside the goods on display in his window. Starting in business on 39 Main Street in 1908, Mr Jones had established himself as a watchmaker and jeweller on King Edward Street by 1912. He later owned premises on both Station Road and Victoria Street.

H. Hardy's saddlery store, Market Place. Harry Hardy appears in the 1908 Kelly's directory as "saddle, harness and horse clothing maker and colliery contractor." Still in business at his Market Place shop in 1916, he had disappeared by the early 1920s.

Beehive Stores, Station Road. The Beehive Stores were founded in 1895 on Station Road, just off the Market Place, under the proprietorship of Mr Mark Robinson. Briefly renamed the "Spirit Glass", in modern times, the store still operates from its original premises as the "New Beehive."

Cottages, Division Road. Now destroyed, the cottages were the homes of Mr Joseph Middleton and his family. The three girls in the picture are (left to right): Audrey Collins, Barbara Staniforth, and Joan Cox (now Mrs Madin).

River Plate Fresh Meat Co., Ltd., 1903. Established in the 1900s, the River Plate Fresh Meat Co., Ltd. first sold from premises at 35 Main Street and 7 King Edward Street. This early picture shows the manager, Mr Joseph Parker (left) who came to Shirebrook from Uttoxeter, and his errand boy George Harrison (right, with basket) with a third, unidentified person in front of the shop. The firm later changed its name to the British and Argentine Meat Co., Ltd., and its address to 12 Main Street, before becoming part of Dewhurst's Butchers. The premises at 35 Main Street were later used as a shoe shop by Herbert Brough.

King Edward Street, with "Gate" Inn. A street first constructed in the 1900s, extending Main Street eastward to join Portland Road, King Edward Street is shown approaching the junction with Victoria Street on the left. To the right is the "Gate" Inn, Shirebrook's oldest working public house, which dates back to the late 18th century.

Co-op and Patchwork Row, 1950s. Part of the original course of Main Street, which had to turn sharply to the left to avoid the buildings later removed to form King Edward Street, Patchwork Row got its name from the varied nature of its shops and house frontages. The large timbered structure on the left is the No.2 branch of the Pleasley and Pleasleyhill & District Co-operative Society, opened in 1924, which is now in use as a District Council office and advice centre.

Market Place, Shirebrook. A 1950s shot from the southern end of the Market Square. Built in the 1900s, it remains one of the largest for a village of Shirebrook's size, and was for many years the favoured site for the annual October "feasts".

Central Drive, Model Village, 1950s. A view from the Model Village side, close to the junction with Main Street. Shirebrook Police Station is set back from the road to the right, and immediately below it the Central Garage founded by Carl Nicholson in 1924.

Victoria Street c.1960. A view along Victoria Street from the Market Place to its junction with Carter Lane. The rows of terraced houses on either side date from the 1920s, and were demolished during the 1980s to make room for a Co-operative store and supermarket. Carter Lane Service Station, which appears in the background, had part of its original structure removed in 1991 to accommodate the Aldi store and car park on the far side of the road. The cars and the parked motorcycle suggest a date around 1960.

A Vanished Prospect: Stinting Lane. A 1950s shot of Stinting Lane, viewed across the open expanse of Carl Nicholson's field from Main Street. The small bungalow between the two houses was the home of the hardware dealer Mr Grainger. The farmland was built over with new housing to form the area known as the Spinney in the 1960s.

Upper Langwith. Seen from the eastern side, following the road from Langwith Bassett to Hillstown. Upper Langwith, a small hamlet adjoining Shirebrook, still preserves a pleasing rural charm. The wooden building (centre right) is the church hall for Holy Cross Church, and the stone structure fronted by milk churns is Church farm. Skylined on the far left is the "Devonshire Arms" public house.

Village green, Nether Langwith. The furthest from Shirebrook of the five separate settlements comprising Langwith, Nether Langwith crosses the border into Nottinghamshire; it is also one of the most attractive. In the foreground the stream, a tributary to the Poulter, runs between village green and road, while behind it stands the "Jug and Class" public house. Very little seems to have changed since this picture was taken in the 1920s, and the green and its pub are still a favourite haunt for summer visitors.

Two

The Colliery

Shirebrook Colliery, 1950s. Taken by Mr Stanley Bettison, this view from Acreage Lane gives a clear perspective of the colliery buildings, the tall chimney and cooling tower, and the twin headstocks backed by the growing spoil heap, or "pit tip".

Prospectus of the Shirebrook Colliery Company Ltd. Circulated to interested parties by the Managing Director, Professor Arnold Lupton, shortly after the founding of the company in 1895.

A Departure is Announced. Professor Arnold Lupton, founder of the Shirebrook Colliery and the man responsible for the creation of the Model Village, announces his resignation as manager in 1899. The decision followed a bitter strike during 1898, when Lupton was obliged to concede his workers' demands for better wages and conditions. The father of modern industrial Shirebrook, Professor Lupton later became M.P. for Sleaford, Lincolnshire.

No.1 Winding house, Shirebrook colliery. An early interior shot of the winding house, with the winding engine built by Markham & Co., of Chesterfield. Said to be capable of raising a 5-ton dead load from a depth of 550 yards at 70 winds per hour, No.1 winding engine sent down 6 empty tubs on its double deck and raised 6 full loads from the shaft.

No.1 Winders, Langwith colliery. An older colliery than Shirebrook, Langwith was sunk in 1876 by the Sheepbridge Coal and Iron Company. The winding engine at the downcast shaft was vertical with two cylinders 40" in diameter by 6' stroke, that at the upcast slightly smaller, with two horizontal cylinders. The photograph was taken by Mr Frank Grime in the 1930s. Langwith Colliery was closed in September 1978.

Colliery wood shop, c. 1900. Here wood was sawn and shaped to required sizes for use as props, cappers and shuttering in the underground workings. In the early days, before metal superseded timber, the wood shop was of particular importance to the colliery operations.

Colliery machine shop c. 1900. Repair and replacement of colliery equipment was carried out in the machine shop, where tubs, lockers and other items were built or maintained. The shop at one time included a smithy for the shoeing of the pit ponies.

Colliery screens. Powered by a 130 horsepower twin compound engine, the screens were purchased from Clench & Co. of Chesterfield, some time between 1896 and 1900, at a cost of £258. Workers had to sort the coal by hand as it passed over the conveyer, an arduous task.

Installing steam boiler, Shirebrook colliery. This photograph, which must date from the late 1890s, shows the installation of one of several large steam boilers above the "fireholes" which provided the necessary heat. Between them, boilers like this developed the steam power on which the entire colliery was run - winding machinery, heating and the generating of electricity for light all depended on the steam for their operation.

Damaged kibble at surface, 1897. A graphic close-up of a wrecked haulage bucket, or "kibble", taken soon after it broke from its rope and plunged into the colliery shaft. One unfortunate man lost a foot as a result, but it could have been much worse; seventeen miners were at the bottom of the shaft, and were narrowly missed by the falling bucket.

126

CAGE ACCIDENT, SHIREBROOK COLLIERY, DERBYSHIRE.

MESSRS. J. WADSWORTH AND T. RICHARDS' REPORT.

To the Chairman and Members of the Executive Committee of the Miners' Federation of Great Britain.

GENTLEMEN,

In accordance with your instructions, we attended the inquest upon the victims of the Shirebrook Colliery Shaft Disaster, which occurred upon the 26th day of March, 1907, in which the following three workmen lost their lives :—Arthur Barton, single ; William Limb, married ; William Phillips, married.

The inquest was opened upon April 4th, 1907, at the Victoria Hotel, Shirebrook, before Coroner Dr. Green. Sir William Clegg, Solicitor to the Derbyshire Miners, appeared on our behalf; the Colliery Company and Officials were represented by Mr. H. A. Saunders, Solicitor, Mr. W. B. Hextale, Barrister, and Mr. Binns, Secretary of the Colliery Owners' Indemnity Association ; Mr. T. E. Ellis, Barrister, Messrs. A. M. Wilson and A. J. Bailey, represented the National Amalgamated Union of Labour. There were also present: Messrs. A. H. Stokes and D. H. Hepplewhits, H.M. Inspectors of Mines; Mr. William Harvey, M.P., and Mr. Barnett Kenyon, Miners' Agents; and the two Checkweighers at the colliery.

The No. 2 Shaft, in which the accident occurred, is the upcast, and is only used for winding workmen and the necessary materials for use at the collieries, the whole of the coal being raised through the downcast shaft, No. 1.

The shaft is 544 yards deep, fourteen workmen ride at the time in a single-deck cage.

As a large number of witnesses were called, and extensively examined, we do not think more than a brief summary of the facts elicited is necessary in this report, inasmuch as there can be no doubt as to the immediate cause of the accident.

When the cage was descending with the full complement of workmen, viz: fourteen, about 5·40 a.m., one of the wire rope

Cage accident, 1907. Opening page of the official report on the Shirebrook cage accident of March 26th 1907, when three miners fell to their deaths. A wire rope conductor fouled or "sluffed", tilting the cage and hurling the men down the shaft. The worn condition of the conductor was noted by the inspectors, who suggested that the fitting of a gate to replace the loose bar on the cage would probably have saved the men.

34

Colliery rescue teams. With only the most rudimentary safety precautions being taken in the mines in the early 20th century, accidents deaths were common. In Shirebrook Colliery's first ten years of production, there were 16 fatalities. Rescue teams like these were constantly in action, and required men of exceptional skill and courage. The uniformed man in both photographs is Mr J.G. Huskisson, superintendent from 1909 to 1929.

St. John's Ambulance Class, Shirebrook Colliery, July 1952. Members of the Shirebrook Colliery St. John's Ambulance Class, photographed on the premises in the summer of 1952. A presentation to all members who achieved 100% passes in the 1951-52 examinations was made at the Colliery Canteen on July 5th by Mr J.T. Rice, Northern Area Commissioner for the St. John's Ambulance Service, and the Secretary-Instructor was W.D. Taylor. Office and canteen buildings are to the left, the large water cooling tower (dated 1949) to the right. Among those present are, Back row: Joe Bennett (2nd left), Ken Rogers (6th left). 3rd row: Frank Barnes, Jim Conlon, Jim Lambert, Roland Jones, Albert Moore, Jim Pickbourne, Harry Pegg, Harry Easter, Joe Carrington, Stan Carter, Archie Machin, Walt Turner, Billy Press. 2nd row: Cyril Burden (2nd left), Dixon Taylor (5th left), Ted Hawson, Dennis Shepherd, Arthur Cooper, Bill Cox, George Hardy, Harry Roberts, Jock Palmer, Harry Shaw, Ted Machin, Harry Boffin, Joe Pickbourne, Alf Young (18th left), Eric Perkins, George Edwards, Jack Turton *, George Taylor, Fred Saunders, Jack Turton (25th left) *, Fred Jackson (27th left), Harold Collis, Harold Smith. Front row (seated): Joe Holland, George Wells, Bill Carrington, Jack Mellors (5th left), Mr Parry, manager (7th left), Seth Oakton (10th left).

* N.B. There are two candidates called Jack Turton in the picture.

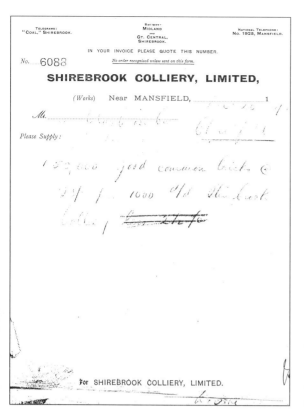

Shirebrook colliery handbill. An order to the Clay Cross Company for 150,000 "good common bricks", written four years after sinking operations commenced in 1896.

Miners in No.51 headings, Shirebrook Colliery. Front row (left to right): Freddie Holland, Harry Roberts, Mr Thompson (manager), Jack Mellors (N.U.M. branch president). Back row (left to right): Maurice Denham, Joe Collier, unknown, Billy Biggs, ? Felse, Harvey Webster, Johnny Ryan.

Winding controls, Shirebrook Colliery. Max Wood at the computer console controlling the winding gear, in an interior shot from the 1960s.

The fall of the Colliery chimney, 1981. The chimney at Shirebrook Colliery had been part of the Model Village skyline from the late 1890s, and was reputed to be the tallest in the county. Its destruction in 1981 marked the end of an era.

Pit ponies at grass, 1934. Like most other collieries, Shirebrook made extensive use of pit ponies for haulage work underground. The animals spent most of their lives in the mine, and no doubt relished their brief spells of freedom in the fresh air above the surface. During the Pit Holiday Week the ponies were brought out to grass, and are here seen taking their ease, with the houses of Field Drive and Recreation Drive in the background. In later years the field was built over to provide the bungalows that are now part of Field Drive and Briar Close.

Last pit ponies leaving the colliery. The last ponies to work in Shirebrook Colliery are led out from the tunnel on May 18th 1971, watched by children and teaching staff from the Park Infants School. Among those present are Mrs P. Henry, headmistress (2nd row, 4th left), colliery official Mr E. Cook (5th left) and Mr Simon Hill (far right).

Production Record, December 1970. A group of Shirebrook miners pose for the camera in front of a loaded tub inscribed with their achievement, the turning of a second million tons of coal one week before the schedule, on 11th December 1970. Jack Smith, the N.U.M. branch president, is in the foreground, and behind him (with hats raised) are Frank Graves (front) and Norman Wall. Closer to the tub (in striped shirt) is Bob Hurst. Scenes like these were typical of Shirebrook Colliery in its productive prime. Sadly, the recent closure of the pit has relegated Shirebrook's long history as a mining village to a fond memory, and such days are firmly part of the past.

Three
Road and Rail

Langwith Junction Railway Station. The busiest station on the Lancashire, Derbyshire and East Coast Railway, Langwith Junction was established in 1897. It formed a junction with the Beighton branch line, through which links were later made with the Midland and Great Central Railways. Renamed Shirebrook North in 1924, Langwith Junction in its heyday was a thriving centre employing many workers. The four-platformed station included a refreshment room and locomotive shed. The 1950s picture shows the imposing nature of the station complex, with the houses of Langwith Road and Burlington Avenue silhouetted in the background. Passenger traffic on the line was discontinued in 1964, and the station has since long disappeared.

Midland Railway Station (Shirebrook West). The Mansfield-Worksop line of the Midland Railway, constructed in 1875, was Shirebrook's first railway line, passing the then small farming settlement on its eastern side to continue further north. It remained unrivalled for more than 20 years, when the Lancashire, Derbyshire and East Coast Railway and the Great Northern Railway arrived at the turn of the century. Passenger traffic had ceased by the 1960s, and the station is nowadays used only as a repair depot, but the station building still stands, and retains its period charm. Here we see it in earlier, happier times.

The engine driver. Shirebrook engine driver Frank Allsop, with unknown passenger, halts his locomotive en route to Clipstone Junction to be photographed.

Midland Station (Shirebrook West). A more recent shot c. 1950, with a locomotive passing under the bridge to enter the station, and a soldier in full kit waiting on the platform.

Shirebrook colliery sidings. A view from early in the century, showing the pattern of tracks leading by the full weigh office to the left, where coal was weighed and sorted. The "Red Bridge", a famous local landmark, spans the line in the background. The waggons in the sidings, marked with the name of the Shirebrook Colliery Company, were built on site by Edward Eastwood of Chesterfield.

Langwith Junction Station, with steam and diesel trains. A unique photograph from the summer of 1958, which shows a diesel multiple unit on its only visit to Shirebrook station from Lincoln, to carry the children of the Langwith Junction Mission Sunday School on a seaside outing to Mablethorpe. The steam locomotive on the right is of a 1912 type, used for many years to service local collieries from their base at Langwith Junction Engine sheds.

Shirebrook's Iron Road. Another view of the Langwith Junction railway network in the 1950s. The main signal-box is in the left foreground, while to centre right the small domed building is the platelayer's cabin, adjoined by the larger cabin for the wiremen. In the distance the line continues south and east towards Warsop in neighbouring Nottinghamshire.

Sir Nigel Gresley. At the Shirebrook Midland Depot Open Day, 1987.

Flying Scotsman. At Shirebrook North (Langwith Junction) station, during the Great Central Rail Tour of 1968.

Aboard the Flying Scotsman. The late Mr Reginald Thompson, parish church choirmaster and long-serving railwayman, takes the controls during the Great Central Rail Tour of 1968, at Shirebrook North (Langwith Junction) station.

Truman's first omnibus, Station Hotel. William Truman started in business as a greengrocer with premises on Station Road some time before 1912, but expanded his activities to take in the running of a passenger omnibus service. Established as a fully licensed operator in 1932, Mr Truman was involved in horse-drawn transport at a much earlier stage. Here his original horse-drawn omnibus waits outside the Station Hotel with a group of passengers. The man in the boater, holding his coat over his arm, is Mr Percy Cooke, who was killed in a mining accident at Warsop Main Colliery in 1920.

Isaiah Glover and his omnibus, 1926. Isaiah Glover first appears in local directories as a shopkeeper in 1912. He quickly established himself as head of a coal and coke delivery business with premises on Victoria Street in the centre of the village. His other enterprises included the first licensed omnibus service to be based in Shirebrook, which in 1926 secured official approval to carry passengers from Shirebrook to Mansfield via the Sookholme route. Mr Glover is seen pictured between his two employees Harry Stubbs (left) and Ernest Humphries (right) with their vehicle, an American Maxwell bus previously used by Lord Savile as a shooting-brake, parked on the open ground to the rear of Victoria Street and Market Street. The building directly behind the bus is Hodgson's bakery.

Glover's second omnibus. Mr Glover's driver, William "Wiggy" Mee, is shown with his sister Edith Mee in front of the Model T Ford omnibus. This vehicle carried Shirebrook women to work at Pleasley Vale Mills in the mornings and evenings, and the resourceful Mr Glover converted the bus for coal deliveries during the day! The stables behind the bus were used to house the coal cart horses.

Truman's buses, 1. A double-decker drawn up at the Market Place bus stop, opposite the Market Hotel or "Drum". Note the folded market stalls, which were stored on this side of the road ready for erecting on market days. The photograph probably dates from the early 1950s.

Truman's buses, 2. Another double-decker, parked on open ground on the unmade part of the Market Square, 1950s.

Rest stop. Truman's single-deck coach on the Warsop-Shirebrook route, 1950s. The conductress is May Wardle.

Terminus. Fred Cooke, with his single-decker Crossley coach at Shirebrook Bus Station, Carter Lane, in the 1950s.

Truman's bus crews, 1950s. Back row (left to right): Jim Hall, Tom Molineux, Mev Warriner, Harry Stubbs, Bob Whitstead, Mick Smithard, Bill Sturley, Luther Harper, Sam Mee, Frank Winter, Bill Vassie. Front row (left to right): George Swain, Tom Mellard, Pete Hodgetts, Dick Dillon, Dennis Youd, Frank Wood.

Truman's bus service: driver and conductor. Ivan Amos (left) and Syd Boden (right) face the camera in this 1950s shot.

No.73, Market Place. Truman's eventually sold out the company to East Midland Motor Services in 1956, and most of the vehicles were destroyed. They were replaced on the familiar routes by double-decker buses of the kind shown here. This No. 73 was one of several that ran a regular service from Shirebrook to Mansfield, as Truman's buses had done before.

Twilight of the gods. William Truman established a thriving transport company, and when he finally sold out to East Midland Motor Services in 1956 he owned a fleet of over 50 buses. Unfortunately most of the vehicles were reckoned unfit for service, and their former owner had them lined up on waste ground fronting the railway banking, where many of them were burned and their engine blocks destroyed. The pictures above and below show the single-decker and double-decker coaches awaiting their end after years of service.

Four
Work and School

Carl Nicholson's Central Garage, 1924. Carl Nicholson (2nd from left) supervises refuelling of a car and motorcycle at his newly opened garage on Central Drive in 1924. Mr Nicholson, a descendant of the well-known farming family of Shirebrook, established the business after returning from army service in World War I.

In service. Miss J. Turton and Miss Gilbert, photographed in their maids' uniforms while in service at William Hollins & Company's textile mills at Pleasley Vale, c. 1900.

A Shirebrook nanny. Mrs A. Stephenson, wife of Mr Arthur Stephenson, in her nanny's uniform, in September 1920.

Shirebrook's first police sergeant. Sergeant James Brown, described as "sergeant in charge" in a 1904 trades directory, headed the forces of law and order during Shirebrook's early years as a mining "boom town". He supervised four constables, and had responsibility for the running of the newly built police station with its two cells. His wife was paid 2/- for the dubious privilege of delousing female prisoners!

Frank Martin, special constable. Taken during the Second World War. The chevrons reflect Mr Martin's previous service as an army sergeant in World War I. He also worked as caretaker of the Colliery "Top Offices" and the Model Village Recreation Ground.

Under observation. P.C. Patrick Tierney subjects the stock of Carl Nicholson's Central Garage to a thorough investigation in this 1950s shot.

Nurse Quemby and her daughter. Nurse Quemby was born in India, where she married a British serviceman and later came to England. She first took up residence in Shirebrook in 1927, having trained as a nurse. Shirebrook's first official midwife, she became a well-known and respected figure in a career spanning the 1930s-1950s. Nurse Quemby is on the left of the picture, with her daughter Hyacinth (now Mrs Robinson) on the right.

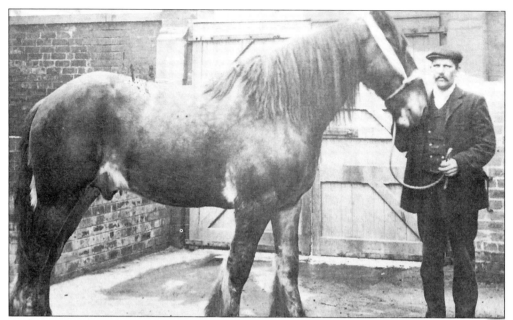

Graham Wood, ostler. Taken outside the stables adjoining the Market Hotel, or "Drum", c.1910. The Market Hotel was established in 1907, and the stables were apparently leased to one of the railway companies (either Great Central or Great Northern) by Shipstone's Brewery. The company stabled two draught horses, and employed two ostlers, Graham Wood and Mr Owen.

Shirebrook Fire Brigade. Firemen and fire engine in a shot taken on the British Rail Staff Association playing field, Langwith Road, during the 1960s.

They had their Weetabix. Fire Brigade members on the Staff Association field, Langwith Road, at a gala or demonstration in the 1960s. Left to right are: Frank Battersby, Mick Fretwell, Alfred Brittles and Ted Fletcher.

Sam Pegg, rat-catcher. One of several Shirebrook "characters", Sam Pegg was active as a professional rat-catcher and unofficial veterinary surgeon from the 1930s to 1950s. He lived in the Langwith Junction area to the east of the village, and is pictured here in his garden with two of his dogs, who frequently accompanied him on his rat-hunting trips. His best-known dog, Prince, achieved fame in his own right by killing a record number of rats.

A Shirebrook ambulance man. Henry Shaw in his ambulance sergeant's uniform, pictured in front of the Shirebrook ambulance station on Park Road.

A landlord and his staff. Frank Baines (far left) and members of his bar staff pose behind the bar of the Market Hotel, more popularly known as the "Drum". The young man third from left is Leonard Ward.

Leech Ices, Park Road. A budding entrepreneur sells ice cream from a home-made barrow along Park Road. The buildings in this area were begun in the early 1920s, and include some of the earliest examples of council housing in Shirebrook. Judging by their pristine state, this picture probably dates from the late1920s or early 1930s.

A milkman's round. Mr Frank Burton halts his horse-drawn milk float outside the "Gate" Inn during his morning round. Mr Burton owned Bath Farm, at nearby Sookholme, from which the milk deliveries were made. The passenger is his employee Mrs Amos, and the picture dates from some time in the 1940s.

Shirebrook entrepreneurs at the Market Hotel. The bowler-hatted gentleman standing in the doorway is John William Moore, who with his brother Frederick Henry Moore was a leading figure in the Shirebrook business community in the period 1900-1930. The Moores built most of the houses in central Shirebrook following the sinking of the colliery in 1897, and were also directors of the Shirebrook Gas Company. F.H. Moore owned the Station Hotel, and J.W. Moore the Market Hotel or "Drum", for which he secured a licence in 1907. Their cousin Mark Robinson managed the Beehive Stores on Station Road, and may have acted briefly as licensee of the Market Hotel. The first regular landlord, Frank Baines, is seated in the front row on the left, while standing 2nd from left is Leonard Ward, who later established a grocery business on King Edward Street. The gentleman in the cap in the front row is Harry Ruggins, who worked as rent-collector for the Moores, and lodged at the Market Hotel before his marriage. The picture dates from around 1910.

"Tubby" Coupe's workforce. A family long established in Shirebrook, the Coupes appear as carpenters and wheelwrights in Census Returns for the old agricultural village. The undertaking business with which they are now associated was located at the bottom of Central Drive, and shared premises with the local blacksmith Levi Elvidge. Frederick Coupe was head of the firm at the time this picture was taken, and the workers shown are (left to right): Frederick Coupe, Jr., Bill Walker, Mr Clay, and Les Howiss. The young boy kneeling in the foreground is Bill Walker's son, Roland Walker.

Mr Martin, civilian. A less formal shot of Mr Frank Martin in the garden of the Colliery Offices, with his dog taking a well-earned rest in the wheel-barrow.

Shirebrook Salvation Army Officers, 1899. The Salvation Army chapel was first established on Byron Street in 1899, and pictured here are the original group of officers assigned to the village. They include Captain Duggins (far left) and Lt. F.A. Boxall (far right).

Model Village Boys, class IV, 1922. Top row (left to right): Tindall ?, Harry Gilbert, Percy Kerry, unknown, B. Wood, Harry Kane, rest unknown. 3rd Row: E. Higgs (3rd left), Clarence Bates, ? Kerry, unknown, Fred Mellors, Cyril Burden, Bill Bonser, Sam Annable, Denis Purseglove, ? Truman. 2nd Row: George Bolton, 2-4 unknown, Eric Wilkinson, Fred Butler, unknown, Joe Collier, Harry Dawkins, 10-11 unknown, Ted Hampson. Front row: Ron Atkin, unknown, Jim Roberts, ? Bryan, Johnny Webmore, unknown, G. Bottom, rest unknown. Teacher: Mr Graham.

Model Village Infants, class 2A, 1915. The Model Village Boys' and Infants' Schools were founded in 1907, and were first run by Enoch Bell and his wife Elizabeth. Mr Bell also served as parish clerk, and as a J.P. The teacher on the left is his daughter Miss Tempest, Miss Alcock is on the right. The child 5th from right on the back row is Harry Gilbert.

Form IV, Shirebrook Girls' Grammar School, 1941. Situated at Langwith Junction, the school was also known as 'Miss Wills's School', and had the R.A.F. motto 'Per Ardua ad Astra'. Back row (left to right): Pat Jerrison, Hyacinth Quemby, Audrey Whittington, Jean Palmer, Margaret Savage, Kitty Nuttal, Iris Johnson, Marion Parker. Middle row: Joan Hurton (now Mrs Mallett), Kathleen Riley (now Mrs Spowage), Audrey Over, Jean Ibbotson, Madge Bennett, Margaret Holmes, Ruth Johnson, Gladys Walker. Front row: Jessie Holland (now Mrs Millward), Eunice Giles, Barbara Packman, Norma Kirk, Winifred Price, ? Wilson, Barbara Rodgers, Joyce Holden.

Carter Lane School Class c.1900. One of the earliest photographs of Carter Lane pupils and staff in the classroom, shortly after the building was established as a Board School in the 1890s.

Carter Lane Boys' School football team. This side won the East Derbyshire Boys' League in 1934-35, and were losing finalists to Whitwell Boys in the East Derbyshire Teachers' Charity Cup. Standing to the right is Carter Lane headmaster Thomas 'Daddy' Reay, who was president of the Shirebrook Town Football Club in the late 1920s.

Shirebrook Central School footballers. Members of the 1st eleven, 1929-30 season, soon after the school was opened on Langwith Road in 1929.

A school trip. Shirebrook Model Village Boys' School pupils at Cromford Dam, on a trip from Amber Valley Camp, c. 1960.

Carter Lane Boy's School, 1928. Back row (left to right): Albert Williamson, ? Walker, Len Spencer, unknown, Ken Doan, ? Moon, ? Gellatly, Steel, ? Oxley, unknown, Eric Brocklehurst, Bob Hibberd, others unknown. 3rd row: unknown, ? Corcoran, Ken Rodgers, Jim Brett, Len Gough, ? Carlin, Eric Hardy, unknown, Dick Dillon, unknown, ? Flowers, ? Hall, unknown, ? Goodwin. 2nd row:Thomas 'Daddy' Reay (headmaster), Austin Webster, Vic Parkin, unknown, Alec Hall, ? Hancock, Fred King, Walter Woolley, unknown, ? Jones, Doug Speed, ? Davies, ? Taylor, next two unknown, Miss Packman (teacher). Front row: Charlie Cooper, next two unknown, ? Else, Jack Gorrill, unknown, Fred Scott, last two unknown.

Star pupils, 1945. Members of class 4A, Carter Lane. Back row (left to right): Barry Clarke, Keith May, Arthur Morley, John Floyde, Eric Potts, Raymon Wilson, Ted Hazlehurst, Alan Warriner, John Carrier, Alan Sheperd, ? Brickles, Victor Crew. Middle row: Mrs Hudson (teacher), Ted Taylor, Tony Saunderson, Robin Oakton, Lawrence Barnes, Alfred Williamson, Roy Hallam, John Martin, Michael Higginson, ? Cooper, John Howe, unknown, Terry May, unknown, Mr Atkin (headmaster). Front row: Trevor Blackwell, Harry Roberts, unknown, Jeff Tomlison, Colin Palmer, Edgar Layton, Geoffrey Cox, Graham Miller, Brian Johnson, Tony Tuffrey, Alan Reddish. (Raymon Wilson is better known as Ray Wilson, the England left-back in the World Cup winning team of 1966).

Unemployed workers at Sookholme, 1936. During the period of the Depression in the 1930s, there were many who found it hard to obtain work of any kind. Shirebrook's Unemployed Workers, who included a number of Communist Party members, were among those who campaigned for the right to work. They posed for this group portrait under the arches of the Sookholme viaduct prior to joining the Jarrow marchers on their journey to London. The man with his arm raised is Mr Greenwood, a prominent local Communist. Also present are Sol Howard (back row, far right), Billy Green (2nd row, seated, far left) and Danny Crew, the drummer on the far right, who was awarded the Military Medal in the First World War.

Railway waggon repair team, Shirebrook Colliery, 1938. Unlike many subsidiary functions carried out by Shirebrook Colliery itself, the company's railway waggons were built and maintained by the Chesterfield-based firm of Edward Eastwood & Son, whose Shirebrook depot was located at the pit top. The group of painters and repairers shown here are (back row, left to right): George Slaney (sign writer), Hector Chambers (waggon repairer), Tom Swinscoe (apprentice painter, later professional footballer with Chesterfield F.C.), Bernard Hallam, Jr. (apprentice waggon repairer), Stan Rowbottom (waggon repairer), Dick Barlow (waggon repairer). Front row, left to right: Ron Gilbert (apprentice painter), Bernard Hallam, Sr. (shop foreman), Joe Hallam (apprentice waggon repairer). The boy in the foreground is Jim Pickbourne, also an apprentice waggon repairer.

Five

People at Play

Youth Club Christmas, 1950s. Malcolm Shaw, in unusual festive garb, at St Joseph's Church Hall, Langwith Road, taking part in the Shirebrook Youth Club's Christmas celebrations.

The pleasures of camping. A sequence of shots from the late 1930s, when the Shaw family and Shirebrook scouts camped at Tagg's farm, Church Road, Skegness. Mr and Mrs Henry Shaw at ease in their tent.

Shirebrook scouts raise the flag above the campsite.

74

An unguarded moment, with camera-shy subject.

A family close-up. Malcolm Shaw is the child in the foreground. The others are (left to right): Cliff Jones, Cyril Jones, Mrs Anne Shaw, Bill Shaw, and Humphrey Williams.

Salvation Army outing, 1920s. A largely female group, possibly members of the Home League, with children and babies, prior to departure. Their formidable expressions and daunting array of hats match the almost armour-plated, military aspect of the charabanc in which they are travelling.

Baby show, Derbyshire Miners' Holiday Camp, Skegness, 1950. Prizewinners (left to right): Mrs H. Perkins (standing), unknown, Mr F. Bown, Miss Dillon, Holiday Queen (standing), Mrs Emma Roberts with daughter Linda (seated, centre), unknown, Mrs Greenhill, Mrs D. Beresford (standing).

Holiday group, 1930s. Adults and children, among them members of the Shirebrook Scout Troop, in a collective pose at their Skegness camp site. Drinks are strategically placed in the foreground.

Happy wanderers. Scouts board a farm cart for an unorthodox group portrait, before exploring the Lincolnshire countryside.

Shirebrook No.333 Scout Troop, 1930s. A Salvation Army Scout Troop, photographed in camp with banner and drums, some time in the 1930s. Those present include (back row, left to right): Harry Gilbert (scoutmaster), Frank Edge (3rd left), Billy Leadbeater, Ernest Wagstaffe, ? Fuller. Middle row: George Leadbeater (3rd left). Front row: ? Randall, ? States (3rd left), Charlie Wall (4th left). Charlie Wall later achieved success as a trumpeter and dance band leader.

The roar of the crowd. A group of Shirebrook football fans immortalised by the camera while watching a cup-tie between Shirebrook and Boston United, probably during the 1952-53 season. Boston eventually won a close-fought contest by three goals to two. Among those pictured are Frank Dunstan (7th from right), Dennis Kerley (6th), Ernest Dunstan (5th), Jock Middleton (4th, in cap), Mrs M. Moore (3rd), Mrs Priest (2nd), and Mrs Smith (far right). Behind Frank Dunstan is Stan Smith (in cap), and behind Ernest Dunstan is Mr Duckworth, while behind Mrs Moore and Mrs Priest (left to right) are Fred and Marion Widdowson, and Fred Goddard (in glasses and cap). The match was played on the Langwith Road Ground.

Model Village cyclists, 1934. Tommy Swinscoe (left) and his friend Ted Wheeler (right) on their bikes at the back of Field Drive, in the Model Village. Tommy Swinscoe was later to win fame as a footballer with Shirebrook Supporters and Chesterfield F.C.

Shirebrook Pit Week at Derbyshire Miners' Holiday Camp. The Derbyshire Miners Holiday Camp at Skegness was the traditional summer venue for Shirebrook miners and their families during the annual Pit Week vacation. Among the crowd in this 1950s photograph are Wilf Bown (centre, with young girl on shoulders) and Joan Cox, now Mrs Madin (smiling, centre foreground).

Mystery trip. A group of Shirebrook miners pose with their uniformed omnibus or charabanc drivers on an unidentified outing from early in the century.

Liquid refreshment. Shirebrook friends on a convivial night out. Left to right: Mr Ashton, Bill Shaw, Mrs Margaret Shaw, Doris Stockdale, Mrs Ashton. At the front of the group, facing the camera, is Ambrose Stockdale.

Holiday athletics, c.1950. Flat race, Skegness beach.

Holiday athletics, c.1950. Egg and spoon race, Skegness beach.

The men and the boys. A group of Shirebrook youngsters show off their manly frames in this pre-war pose, on holiday at Skegness.

Shirebrook holidaymakers, 1950s. A group portrait of adults and children at the Miners' Holiday Camp.

Central Dance Hall, Main Street, 1935. Situated on the corner of 'Patchwork Row' where it joins Carter Lane, the Central Dance Hall was one of the main local venues for dancers during the period 1930-1960. This picture was taken at the time of the celebrations in honour of King George V and Queen Mary's Silver Jubilee in 1935, and shows the wooden building decorated to full advantage. On the far left, in the background, is the original Shirebrook Ex-Servicemen's Club on Carter Lane, also suitably decorated. The Central Dance Hall remained in regular use through the '50s and '60s. Those who attended recall that segregation of males and females was enforced, with two separate entrances and cloakrooms, each supervised by an attendant of the appropriate sex. The hall has now been replaced by a modern Salvation Army church building.

Dancing partners, 1950s. Malcolm Shaw and his partner, Miss Jessie Dean, at a dance held at St. Joseph's Roman Catholic Church Hall, Langwith Junction, during the 1950s.

Miss Mansfield outside tennis pavilion, Model Village, 1930s. The pavilion, situated at the back of Prospect Drive, was for the exclusive use of a tennis club formed by the Thompson family, resident at "The Hollies". The select membership, which included Dr Strevens and the colliery manager Mr Herbert Knighton, paid an annual fee of £1 10s. for the privilege. At a later stage subscriptions were reduced to 10/6d., and colliery office staff were permitted to join. Mr Thompson's daughters, Ethel and Lucy, were keen tennis players, and co-opted Miss Mansfield to form a three-woman team that competed in a number of local tournaments. Miss Mansfield, as Mrs Moore, later taught at the Carter Lane and Model Village schools.

A wandering minstrel.

'I once had a uke-banjolele with George
Formby's name on the vellum
I could strum it real good — it must be in my
blood
(I heard that. Who said: 'He can tell 'em'?)

Ernest Roberts, Shirebrook author, historian,
song-writer, musician, performer and raconteur,
on holiday in Skegness in 1949, provides his
individual version of the Donkey Serenade.

A song for Shirebrook. Ernest Roberts
shows off his vocal talents while on
holiday at the Pier Hotel, Skegness,
during the 1970s.

Motor-cyclists at the Model Village. Joe Mansfield tries out an early Harley-Davidson motor-cycle on waste ground behind Prospect Drive, in the Model Village. The passenger is his father, William Mansfield. Joe, who worked in the Shirebrook and Welbeck Colliery offices, was the father of Miss Margaret Mansfield, later Mrs Moore.

Gentlemen of leisure, Victoria Hotel. Taken in the yard of the Victoria Hotel, the only public house in the Model Village, during the 1940s. Left to right: Fred Madin, Bob Wilson (landlord), Mr Edwards, unknown, 'Packy' Pitchford. 'Packy', a mole-catcher and famed local character, was the father of cyclist Eddie Pitchford.

Holiday group. A group of Shirebrook tourists smile for the camera outside their hotel in this shot, probably from the 1970s. At the centre (in dark blazer) is Mr Henry Shaw, with Mrs Anne Shaw to his right, and further along (4th and 3rd from right) are Mr and Mrs Samuel Bennett.

A giant step. A young Malcolm Shaw encounters the sea for the first time, while on holiday at Blackpool in 1937.

Six
Musical Offerings

Musicians in concert, Empire Theatre. The performers on stage on the opening night of Thomas Moorley's 'Empire Theatre', Station Road, in 1910. The double-bass player on the far left is John Enoch Eccleshall, while the pianist third from left is Ezra Read, whose music compositions sold worldwide, and who spent his last years in Shirebrook.

Shirebrook Comrades' Band. Shirebrook Comrades' Band was formed early in the 1930s, and consisted mainly of boy musicians who practised parades in Shirebrook and Scarcliffe, organised by Mr and Mrs Tom Bills, and Mr T. Foulds, under the title Shirebrook Comrades' Temperance Band (the word 'Temperance' was later dropped from the title). The Comrades practised in a slaughter-house behind Mr A. Neale's shop on Main Street, above which was Mr Wood's billiard hall. At a later stage they moved to more appetising quarters at the Great Northern Hotel, and from there to the upstairs room of the 'Gate' Inn. The band thrived during the late 1930s, but broke up around 1940 due to the loss of musicians called up for military service. Those who remained joined Joseph Levick's Silver Prize Band. Back row (left to right): T. Foulds (bandmaster), H. Bradley, J. Jarrett, G. Ainsworth, O. Hollis, W. Mason, F. Woolley, W. Hutchinson, F. Smith, H. Merry (bandmaster after T. Fould's death), T. Bills. Middle row: G. Kelly, W. Allen, T. Bowsher, A. Brickles, D. Neale, G. Thomas, S. Bowsher, W. Neale, E. Easter, O. Hollis. Front row (kneeling): B. Bills, 'Hodgie', S. Gorrell.

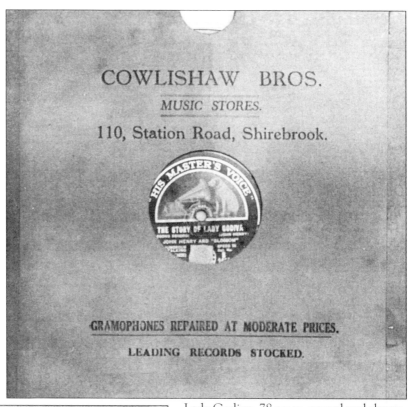

Lady Godiva. 78 r.p.m. record and sleeve, bearing the imprint of Cowlishaw's Music Store, 110 Station Road. The shop which was a favourite haunt of music lovers during the 1920s, finally closed in 1932.

Joseph Levick, musician. An early photograph, showing Shirebrook's first Salvation Army bandmaster as a young musician, his chest emblazoned with the 'Blood and fire' slogan, posing with euphonium at the ready for his portrait.

Joseph Levick, bandmaster. The first bandmaster of Shirebrook Salvation Army band in 1903, Joseph Levick also directed his own band, and in later years achieved fame as bandmaster and conductor of the Shirebrook Silver Prize Band, which won awards at national competitions at Crystal Palace in 1921 and 1931, and at the Albert Hall in 1958. Shown here in his uniform of bandmaster to the Shirebrook Silver Prize Band, Mr Levick was a respected local figure. He died in 1954, and the band accompanied his coffin in the funeral procession through Shirebrook.

Shirebrook Band at Durham Miners' Gala, 1947. Members of the band follow the N.U.M. banner in procession past the Royal County Hotel in the year of the Nationalising of the coal industry. Clement Attlee, Labour's post-war Prime Minister, waves from the balcony.

Prize presentation. Mr Les Lee accepts the award of 3rd prize, 3rd section, from Professor Edmund Rubbra, Master of the Queen's Music, on behalf of the Shirebrook Silver Prize Band, following the National Band Competition of 1958. The competition was held at the Hammersmith Town Hall, and presentations made at the Albert Hall. Mr Lee, now 94 years young, still lives in Shirebrook.

Salvation Army Junior Band, 1930s. Mr J. Heywood, the bandmaster, is seated 3rd from left. The young musicians shown here are (left to right): ? Godfrey, N. Bills, R. Gilbert, D. Benger, V. Crew, J. Footitt, D. Collier, ? Sherwood, I. Bennet, R. Flinders and D. Crew. The girl with the banner at the back of the group is Vera Thompson.

Shirebrook Hillbillies. The group in concert at the Derbyshire Miners' Holiday Camp, Skegness, in 1950. Left to right: Ron Gregory (guitar), Mr Duffy (accordion), Aubrey Payne (tambourine), Roland Walker (masked, with washboard), Hector Payne (guitar, leader).

Shirebrook Hillbillies. A second shot from the same 1950 performance. Left to right: Mr Duffy (accordion), Ron Gregory (guitar), Aubrey Payne (tambourine), Ernest Roberts (banjo?) and Hector Payne (guitar, leader). Ernest Roberts recalls that the over-enthusiastic concert secretary would have liked a campfire in the hall to add atmosphere, but was dissuaded from burning the venue down by the performers!

The Peers and the Peris, Central School, 1951. Pupils of the Shirebrook Central School, in their 1951 performance of Gilbert and Sullivan's *Iolanthe*.

Charlie Faulkner (1899-1964). Charlie Faulkner worked as a coal-miner at Warsop Main before establishing himself as a musician and entrepreneur. He rented the Portland Road football ground from Tennent's Brewery, and ran it as a greyhound track, also organising trotting races at another stadium in Mansfield Woodhouse. A violinist and bandleader from the 1920s, he was owner and resident performer at the Elite Ballroom on Main Street, where his band played for the dancers for over thirty years.

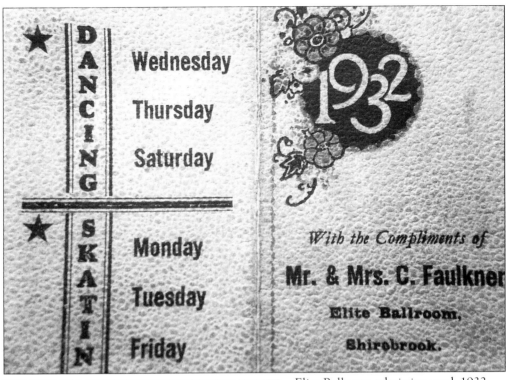

Elite Ballroom admission card, 1932. The Elite Ballroom on 'Patchwork Row' (Main Street) was one of the main dancing venues in Shirebrook until the 1960s. Charlie Faulkner, the bandleader and a prominent local character, provided the music, and dancing alternated with roller skating, each for three nights a week. This attractive admission card from the 1930s indicates the widespread appeal the Elite held for local dancers.

Mr York outside the 'Gate', 1930s. A well-known Shirebrook personality and a member of the 'Black and Ambers' Shirebrook Jazz Band formed in the late 1920s, Mr York strikes a pose by his drum in front of the 'Gate' Inn on King Edward Street. His hat, and the horn carried under his arm, are home-made items produced from cardboard.

Seven
Sport and Sportsmen

Shirebrook Foresters, 1918-19. The trainer on the far left is Mr James Henry Hadlington, who for more than twenty years was associated with several leading Shirebrook sides. The players are (back row, left to right): F. Chambers (later of Bolton Wanderers, right-back), Hadlington (goalkeeper), Ernest 'Mac' England (left-back, later of Sunderland F.C.). Middle row: Cantrell, Tremelling, Slaney. Front row: Spiby, Hadlington, Fretwell, Albert 'Labber' Smith (later of Blackpool) and Griffiths.

Colliery cricket ground c.1900. The Shirebrook Colliery Cricket Club was established in 1899, and their matches played on the ground shown here. The informal dress suggests a game between colliery workers, rather than an official encounter, and probably dates from the turn of the century.

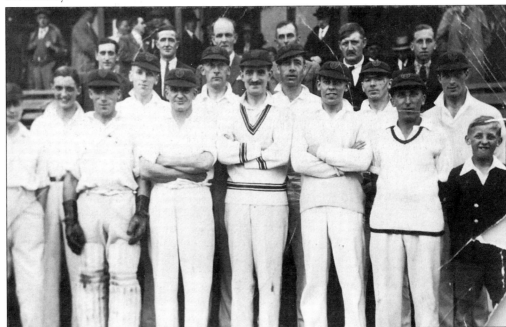

Shirebrook Colliery Cricket Club. Rayner Cup winners, 1932. The Rayner Cup was the knockout competition for teams in the Derbyshire League, and the final was played at Queen's Park, Chesterfield. In all Shirebrook won the trophy six times between 1923 and 1942. Back row (left to right): Dave Griffiths, J. Allen, Robert Collins (secretary), H. Murt, S. Darby (bag carrier), G. Revill, Jr. Middle row: Ron Hays, Howard Goddard (also goalkeeper for Shirebrook F.C. and Aston Villa), J. Shuter, J. Marsden, Fred Turton, C. Wheatley (later headmaster, Langwith Bassett School). Front row: C. Millward, Tom Mitten, Harry Baker, Joe Charlton, A. Drury, George Revill (groundsman). The boy in the foreground is Dick Revill.

Dave Goodwin (1923-1993). Shirebrook's most notable boxer, Dave Goodwin began his career in 1939 at the age of 16, ending it ten years later with a record of 150 fights and only six defeats. This included a run of 27 fights, 26 k.o.'s. Dave fought at middleweight, light heavyweight and cruiserweight, usually topping the bill, for an average purse of £40 (his highest was £50). At the age of 18, in 1941, he was the only professional boxer to have two pro fights in the same night and win them both; this took place at Oxford, and Dave stopped his opponents in 90 seconds and the 5th round respectively. He joined the Grenadier Guards in 1945, and won the regimental heavyweight title with a first-minute knockout in his first twelve weeks in service. Dave's titles as a professional included North Midland Area Light Heavyweight and Middleweight Champion, and undefeated Northern Cruiserweight Champion. Among the 'name' opponents he beat were Jimmy Bray (Lancashire and Cheshire Champion), Driver Hood (Indian Champion; k.o. in 2nd), Gordon Woodhouse (Canadian Champion; k.o. in 4th) and Dick Frame (Irish Champion; points win). All four victories were achieved in 1943. Dave stepped in as a substitute to defeat Jack Johnson, Middleweight Champion of British Guiana, at Walthamstow in 1947, and in the same year stopped Don Cockell at Yeovil in the 8th round. He was one of a select group of fighters to beat Cockell, among them Freddie Mills and Rocky Marciano! For many years a well-known local character, Dave Goodwin died in Shirebrook in 1993.

Shirebrook Football Club, 1919-1920. Shirebrook Football and Athletic Club was formed in 1911, largely at the instigation of John William Moore, the local businessman and councillor who served as club president in the early years. A precursor of the side was active in the 1900s as Shirebrook Moore's Athletic. Shirebrook F.C. played in the Notts. and Derbyshire League before joining the Central Alliance in 1912. They were Alliance Champions in 1913-14, and runners-up the following season and in 1920-21. Established as a limited company in 1922, the club had a 9¼ acre ground on Langwith Road, and changed for matches at the Station Hotel. The team shown outside the 'Station' is the Derbyshire Divisional Cup-winning side of 1919-20, who secured the trophy firstly by a 3-0 victory over New Whittington Exchange, and later drew a bad-tempered replay 2-2 at Staveley, following an objection from their defeated opponents. The cup was once more awarded to Shirebrook when a depleted New Whittington side refused to play extra-time. The line-up includes several future league stars. Back row (left to right): Cottam, Knapton (half-back), Ernest 'Mac' England (full-back, later with Sunderland), Atkins (goalkeeper), D. Jones, Roberts, Bob Ward (full-back, later with Crystal Palace), Tremelling (Blackpool and Preston), and Mr Williamson (trainer and former goalkeeper). Front row: Edwards (outside-right), Giles (outside-right), Winslow, Stanley, Atkins (outside-left). The young mascot in Scottish dress is Mr John McKenzie, who still lives in Shirebrook today.

Warren Terrace Reserves F.C., 1914. Members of the side, on the Warren Terrace playing field. Warren Terrace is the name given to the westermost section of Main Street near the Pleasley Road, and Warren Terrace F.C. was one of the earliest local teams, playing on its own ground and under its own name into the early 1990s.

Muscular Christianity? An unidentified Salvation Army side of 1917, with inscribed match ball.

Shirebrook Villa, 1914-15. One of the many lesser Shirebrook sides, still active in the Shirebrook and District League in the late 1930s.

Shirebrooks Vics, 1929-30. A Model Village team, active in the Sutton and Skegby League during the 1930s. Back row (left to right): G. Rowbottom, Fred Fairburn, ? Harvey, Joe Sargison (goalkeeper), R. Cann, W. Judson, E. Cooper. Middle row: L. Barnes. Front row: J. Wilson, J. Palmer, S. Brazier, M. Welsh, ? Fletcher.

Langwith Colliery Cricket Club 2nd Eleven. Bassetlaw 2nd Division Champions, 1954-55. Back row (left to right): J. Slack, C.Rodway, D. Smith, F. Reeves, N. Jackson, J. Fowler, D. Lee (scorer). Front row: E.Hales, H. Bennett, G. Smith (captain), L. Brown, A. Scofield, R. Woodcock.

Andy Ashton, Motorcycle Champion. Shirebrook motorcycle ace Andy Ashton in action on his Yamaha bike. Andy was Midland Road Racing Champion at 125 c.c. in 1985, and also won the Yeardly Challenge and Prince of Wales trophies in the same year.

Ernest "Mac" England. Perhaps the first of Shirebrook's truly great football players, 'Mac' England had 351 games at left-back with Sunderland F.C. - then one of the country's leading teams - between 1920 and 1930. After a brief stay at West Ham, he ended his impressive career with a further 130 league games with Mansfield Town. A popular figure both in Shirebrook and Sunderland, 'Mac' England died at Radcliffe on Trent in 1982, aged 81.

Mac's cap. A representative cap awarded to 'Mac' England in the 1925-26 season, during his time as regular left-back with Sunderland. As yet unidentified, it is not a Football League or England International cap.

Shirebrook Town F.C., 1927-28. One of the most famous of all Shirebrook football teams, this side topped the Midland League for most of the season against strong opposition from the likes of Nottingham Forest Reserves, Notts. County Reserves, York City, Mansfield Town, and others. Sadly, a bad run of injuries and illness late in the season saw them finish in 8th place, but not before they had secured two minor trophies - the Derbyshire Divisional Cup, with a 2-1 victory over Staveley Town, and the Chesterfield Royal Hospital Cup, defeating Chesterfield 2-0 at Saltergate. Shirebrook are pictured on their home ground adjoining the 'White Swan' public house on Portland Road, in front of the stand built for them by Tennent's Brewery Company in 1926. It was here they met Tranmere Rovers in the 1st round proper of the F.A. Cup in November 1927, fresh from a run of 17 matches with only one defeat, and eight successive victories. Playing in front of a 7,013 crowd, Shirebrook eventually lost 3-1, with goalkeeper Hunt playing out the game with an injured knee, but were by no means disgraced against one of the strongest league sides and their star forward 'Pongo' Waring. Shirebrook's regular line-up for the season consisted of Hunt (goalkeeper), Booton and Slack (full-backs), Barlow (right-half), Evans (centre-half, captain), Mitcham (left-half), Heald (outside-right), Stevenson (inside-right), Binns (centre-forward), Miller (inside-left) and Hopkinson (outside-left). The man in the trilby hat, standing on the far left, is Thomas 'Daddy' Reay, the club president.

Shirebrook Supporters' F.C., 1938-39. Champions of the North Notts. League Division II and winners of the knockout cup in their first season, scoring 87 goals in 22 games. The team played on the White Swan ground formerly used by Shirebrook Town, but later moved to Langwith Road when the stadium became a greyhound track. Back row (left to right): Mr Ball, Abey Hayes, Jim Marriott, Bernard Hallam, Jr. 3rd row: Bill Eaton (secretary), Mr Smith, Selwyn Robinson, ? Kemp, Ernest 'Nigger' Layton, Cyril Palmer, Ron Gilbert, Jim Elms, Fred Julian, Bernard Hallam, Sr. 2nd row: Tom Morley, Mr Hadlington, Ron Hays, Billy Thompson, Audrey Payne (goalkeeper), Bob Hays, Jacky Morgan, Bill Marriott, Sr. Front row: Tom Swinscoe (later of Chesterfield), ? Crowder.

George Harrison, boxer. A popular Shirebrook sportsman, still living in the village. George, who fought at lightweight, had a total of 250 professional bouts in a career spanning the period 1938-53. It included a televised encounter with Ken Barlow (no relation to T.V. actor William Roache!) on the undercard of a programme headlined by another Derbyshire fighter, Peter Bates.

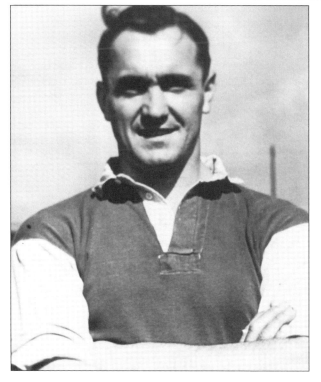

Sammy Chessell. Sammy played local football with Warren Terrace before signing for Mansfield Town as a part-time professional for £1-10s. a week. A regular full-back from 1942-54, he later returned to work at Shirebrook Colliery. Sammy Chessell still lives in Shirebrook.

107

Eddie Pitchford at Crown Farm tournament, 1920s. Shirebrook's most famous cyclist, and a renowned local sportsman, Eddie Pitchford first learned to ride on an old Raleigh cycle, which he bought in 1920 for 6s. 6d. at the rate of 6d. a week. The following year he bought a racing frame fron London, and underwent tuition from his friend Luther Williams, who worked at Shirebrook Colliery. Eddie entered his first race at New Houghton Sports ground, and in 1923 won his first prize in a one-mile contest. He won another one-mile race at Pinxton, and further prizes were collected in the same year, when Eddie also made friends with such Shirebrook and Mansfield riders as Frank Stone, Arthur and Charlie Skelding, Ernest Powell and Wilf Barker. He joined the Ashfield Cycling Club in 1924, and won further awards throughout the 1920s. Eddie was active as a fund-raiser for local miners and their families in the 1926 strike, when he and Ashfield Club rode in the Soup Kitchen Sports on the Model Village Cricket Ground, and also organised a cycle team to play bicycle polo for the soup kitchen collection. The photograph shows a tournament at Crown Farm, in nearby Forest Town, in 1926 or 1927, with Eddie and his pusher Aaron Parker on the right, and his opponent George Tideswell and his pusher Bill Tideswell on the left. (Aaron Parker was also scorer for Shirebrook Colliery Cricket Club). Eddie, who won the 25-mile Time Trial of Great Britain in 1928, and several times defeated the English one-mile champion Harry Wild, is still living in Shirebrook today.

Shirebrook Miners' Welfare Bowls Team, 1974. This team had the distinction of winning the Portland Bowl Trophy (awarded in open competition to the leading bowls club in Nottinghamshire English Bowls Federation affiliated clubs) in two successive years, 1973 and 1974, and suffered its only defeat in the 1975 final. Several members of the side represented the club at county level. Back row (left to right): Mr Collier, A. Melling, J. Collier representing J. Beresford), E. Roberts, E. Mason, G.W. Stevenson. Front row: A. Dennett, M. Stevenson, G. Stevenson, C.A. Oakton (captain), W. Stevenson, E. Cooke.

Tom Swinscoe (1919-1993). One of many talented Shirebrook sportsmen of the 1930s and '40s, Tom Swinscoe attended local shools and began work at Edward Eastwood's waggon repair shop at Shirebrook Colliery as a signwriting apprentice when in his teens. He played his first football for Park Road Rangers and Shirebrook Supporters' F.C. before his career was interrupted by the Second World War. Tom played in distinguished company with a number of Army teams during his infantry service, but lost several years as a potential professional footballer. He was signed by Chesterfield F.C. in 1946, and stayed with them for two seasons before moving to Stockport County in 1948. He also played for several Midland League sides. Afterwards he worked as a fitter at Shirebrook Colliery, and his later occupations included shopkeeper, milkman and poultry station manager. An accomplished inside-forward in his day, Tom Swinscoe died at his home on Vale Drive in 1993.

Ken Wagstaff. Born in the neighbouring village of Langwith, Ken Wagstaff played junior football with Whaley Thorns before attending Carter Lane Secondary School in Shirebrook. He played for Carter Lane, North East Derbyshire, and Langwith Woodland Imps before joining the ground staff at Rotherham United. At 17 he was signed for Mansfield Town, and stayed with them for four seasons. A robust, powerful forward, he scored 105 goals in 196 games for the club. His highest tally, in the 1962-63 season was 41 league and cup goals in 49 games, and helped secure promotion for Mansfield to Division III. Ken moved to Hull City in 1964, and continued to score goals. Joint top scorer in Division IV with 34 league goals for Mansfield in 1962-63, he was also top scorer in Division III for Hull City with 31 goals in 1964-65. He toured Australia with England 'B' in 1971, and ended his career with 307 goals from 554 games. Ken now lives in Hull.

Barry Lyons' father, Joe Lyons, was the star forward and goalscorer with Warren Terrace, and Barry played for Shirebrook Byron Boys from 1959 to 1962 before joining 2nd Division Rotherham United. He moved on to Nottingham Forest in the 1st Division in 1966 and remained there for seven seasons, becoming well-known as a stylish winger in his regular appearances for the 'Reds'. He also played for York City (1973-76) and Darlington (1976-79) before ending his playing career, and managed York City from 1979-81. Barry Lyons now lives in York, where he is co-owner of the St. Mary's Hotel.

Shirebrook Warren Terrace, 1924-25. Back row (left to right): W. Holmes, W. Kitchen, J. Ward, A. Mellor, A. Bennett, A. Stephenson. Middle row: J. Mellor (secretary), J. Dukes, J. Smith, T. Holmes, F. Spencer, E. Shaw (trainer). Front row: F. Hayden, C. Allcott, T. Ward. B. Haydon (captain), B. Haydon (mascot), H. Holmes.

Ray Wilson. Rated the world's best left-back in his day, Ray Wilson is the most famous Shirebrook footballer, and probably its best-known sporting personality. Born in Market Street in 1934, he played for local teams and worked as a waggon repairer and railwayman before making his career in soccer. He won fame with Huddersfield Town and Everton F.C., and earned 63 caps as an England International. Ray was regular left-back in two World Cup teams, including the winners of 1966. He now lives in Yorkshire, where he works as a funeral director.

Ray Wilson as a young player in his Huddersfield days.

Ray in his prime as a regular with Everton F.C.

Pleasley Boys' Brigade F.C., c.1910. Pleasley, a village $2\frac{1}{2}$ miles south-east of Shirebrook, once included the latter within its parish. Though Shirebrook later outstripped Pleasley in size and importance, strong links remain between the two villages. This early shot of a Pleasley football team almost certainly includes some Shirebrook players, as yet unidentified.

Shirebrook Byron Street Football Team, late 1920s. One of the many street teams thriving in Shirebrook in the 1920s and '30s. At one time the village is reputed to have had 24 teams, roughly two for each district. Ernest Smith, one of the players shown, dates this photograph to 1927 or 1928. Back row (left to right): G. Rowbottom, D. York, ? Morley, ? Fanshaw, unknown, Billy Eaton. Middle row: unknown, ? Fleming, ? Steele. Front row: J. Miller, unknown, Ernest Smith, ? Brewin.

Eight
Families and Friends

Gate Yard c.1900. Three well-dressed gentlemen take their ease in the yard of Shirebrook's oldest working public house, some time at the turn of the century.

They also serve. Shirebrook soldiers, photographed while on leave during the First World War.

Two local worthies. A group portrait including Ben Robinson, founder and choirmaster of the Shirebrook Glee Club Singers (back row, 3rd from left) and Herbert White (2nd row, centre) a noted Shirebrook cricketer during the late 1920s, who took over the Warsop Miners' Club in 1939.

A lost Shirebrook Street. A young boy faces the camera in open ground fronting Simpsondale Terrace, which once linked the Market Place to Patchwork Row. The street, demolished in 1968, has now been replaced by the Co-operative Society store car park, the sole reminder being a wall plaque which reads 'Simpsondale Terrace, 1895.'

A Shirebrook smallholder. Mr Arthur Stephenson with his dog, on the smallholding across from his sweet shop. The shop, bought from Mrs Orgill, was a small wooden hut on the fields off Church Drive, approaching the Model Village, and was run by Mr Stephenson during the 1930s.

Mr & Mrs Thomas Moorley at Home Close, Matlock. Born in Derby, Thomas Moorley began his working life as a labourer in a clay pit, but later entered the licensing trade. His arrival in Shirebrook coincided with the rapid growth of the village following the sinking of the colliery, and his own business interests expanded with it, earning him a fortune in the early years of the 20th century. Thomas Moorley held the licence for the Great Northern Hotel on Main Street, and owned Shirebrook's only theatres - the Town Hall (1909) on Main Street, and the Empire (1910) on Station Road; he later operated both venues as cinemas. A keen student of the turf and racehorse owner, Mr Moorley was a respected figure in the community, and a generous benefactor to several deserving causes in Shirebrook and elsewhere. He and his wife moved to Matlock in the 1920s, and are shown outside their house, Home Close on Imperial Road, where Mr Moorley died in 1942, aged 67.

Joseph 'Daddy' Vallance. A well-known character, Joseph 'Daddy' Vallance was a bootmaker in 1899, but this was the least of his many talents. He was a horse and pony dealer, and bought the first palomino pony ever seen in the village, selling it to Mr Bristow for £15. His tar-coated hut, set back from Main Street and subject to flooding, became a landmark, and 'Daddy' himself was noted for his eccentric tastes and unusual inventions. These included a horse-driven cart fronted by a glass windscreen, through which holes were drilled for reins, in order to keep him from getting wet when driving. When he died in 1944, aged 93, he was buried in a coffin of his own design, which enabled him to be interred wearing his top hat!

A Shirebrook Pilot. The son of Shirebrook Glee Club choirmaster Ben Robinson, Flight Sergeant Selwyn Robinson worked as a surveyor at Shirebrook Colliery before serving in World War II as a fighter pilot. He underwent flight training in the United States, and was posted to North Africa, but was tragically killed when the Hurricane fighter he was testing burst into flames in May 1943.

Last resting place. The grave of Flight Sergeant Selwyn Robinson of Shirebrook, somewhere near Benghazi, 1943.

Two grandfathers and their grandchild. Miss Jean Mansfield with her two grandfathers, Mr William Mansfield and Mr William Cooke, taken at the rear of Prospect Drive, Model Village. Behind the group is the header tank of the Model Village Reservoir, which provided the village with its water supply.

Men of leisure, 1930s style. Henry Shaw and his friend Billy Sherwood take it easy on the allotment, some time in the late 1930s.

Harry Thompson. Harry Thompson came to Shirebrook from Edith Weston in Rutland, and is said to have been Shirebrook's first baker. His premises on Nicholson's Row, off Main Street, were later part of Grainger's hardware store. This portrait was taken in 1903 or 1904.

Maggie Weaver. Later Mrs Harland and Mrs Hill, Maggie Weaver was best known to most Shirebrook people by her maiden name, and first arrived in the village as a child of 9 in 1906. A founder-member of the Women's Section of Shirebrook Ex-Servicemen's Club, she was also a member of the British Legion Women's Section and the British Rail Staff Association, and won the affection of local people by her social and fund-raising activities in the 1930s and the 1940s. She ran two carnival bands in the '30s, and later organised children's parties, trips and other social functions. A tireless worker for the village, Maggie Weaver died in 1966, aged 69.

Nellie French and her brothers, Merchant Street. The French family originated from the Tamworth and Fazeley area of Staffordshire, and were typical of many who made the journey from the West Midlands in search of employment at the Shirebrook and Warsop collieries at the turn of the century. Nellie was the first member of her family to be born in Shirebrook, and this picture shows her with her two brothers Basil (left) and Ernest (right) at the family home on Merchant Street, probably in 1913.

Shirebrook church choir. Taken outside Holy Trinity Church some time during the 1930s. Mr Reginald Thompson, the choirmaster, is on the far left. Back row (left to right): Brown, unknown, Allsop, Williams, Stratton, Mrs M. Turton (church organist). Mrs Turton was organist at Holy Trinity church for over forty years, and was awarded the M.B.E. in recognition of her services.

Shipstone's dray in procession, 1950s. Shipstone's Brewery owned the Market Hotel or 'Drum', and part of the adjoining Market Square. This decorated dray with its heavy horses is shown in procession during an unidentified Shirebrook celebration of the 1950s.

Father Braddon and his family. The Rev. Edward Braddon, M.A., was an important figure in Shirebrook during the early part of the present century. His long tenure of office, from 1899 to 1937, spanned the growth of the village from a farming hamlet to a bustling mining community, and involved a memorable confrontation with Arthur B. Markham, M.P., of Stuffynwood Hall, over allegedly 'Romish' religious pictures displayed in the parish church. Mr Markham won that round, but departed soon afterwards, while Father Braddon remained in office for many years afterwards. This Braddon family portrait was probably taken at the Vicarage on Main Street. Back row (left to right): Father Edward Braddon, Kath, Molly and Mary. Front row: Edward, Vera, Paul, Mrs Braddon, Jack and Francie.

Silver Jubilee celebrations, Church Drive. Adults and children in procession down Church Drive in celebration of King George V and Queen Mary's Silver Jubilee in 1935. Harry Roberts, in his ambulance man's uniform, is on the right.

The Flint family of Shirebrook. Family members in a formal pose. William Flint established his butcher's premises on Main Street in the 1890s, and the business continued until bought by Castle Carpets almost a hundred years later in the early 1990s.

Sunday afternoon at 'The Hollies', 1934. Mr Thomas Thompson, who was at various times Secretary and Manager to the Shirebrook Colliery Company, had his private residence at 'The Hollies' on Acreage Lane, in the Model Village. The imposing building stood on its own grounds, and included extensive tennis courts for the use of his twin daughters and their guests. Mr and Mrs Hardy, the gardener and his wife, were often invited to call at the house on Sunday afternoons during the 1930s. This 1934 group consists of Lucy Thompson (far left), and her mother Mrs Thompson (far right), with Mr and Mrs Hardy in the centre of the picture.

VE Day Party, Ashbourne Street. Parents and children pose for the communal photograph between the rows of terraced houses, now hung with flags and decorations. The youngsters seem impatient, and keen to begin the serious business of eating! Ashbourne Street was one of several terraced rows in the middle of the village to be demolished in the early 1970s.

VE Party, Victoria Street. A view along Victoria Street in the last years of World War II, showing the rows of terraced houses, most of which have since been demolished. The residents face the camera prior to the celebration meal, while further back a double-decker bus leaves the Market Place stop en route to Mansfield. The railway embankment, glimpsed in the background, has also since disappeared.

VE Party, Park Road. A group of Shirebrook residents, including adults and children, meet to celebrate victory in Europe in 1945 in the garden of a house on Park Road. Joseph Levick, a well-known local tradesman and character who for many years led the Shirebrook Silver Prize band, is shown on the back row to the left, directly in front of the wooden outbuilding, and the uniformed ambulance man on the right of the group is the late Jack Hunt. The shot provides an interesting view of the rear of the houses off Park Road, with their sheds, fences and entries between buildings, most of which have now been removed to make way for the Kissingate Centre and its grounds. In the distance, on the far left, is the stone bridge that formed part of the Leen Valley extension, another vanished piece of Shirebrook history.